This book belongs to:

. . . . . . . . . . . . . . . . . . . . . .

'Family':
/'famili,'fam(ə)li/
Syn. clan, group, brood, kin, kind...

For our own unique families
— both kin and kind

# We Are Family

Lucy Reynolds & Jenna Herman

# Your family may be big

## Rabbits

Rabbits are pregnant for about five weeks, and can conceive again as soon as their babies are born. Rabbits mate with different partners. In a year they can give birth to four or five litters of six to seven babies, called 'kits' – that's a lot of new siblings joining the colony each year!

## Blue Whales

Blue whales tend to be solitary creatures. Their pregnancies last for almost a year, after which time the mother will give birth to a single baby. She will rear and tend to this calf exclusively, with a space of two to three years before another calf is born.

or small,

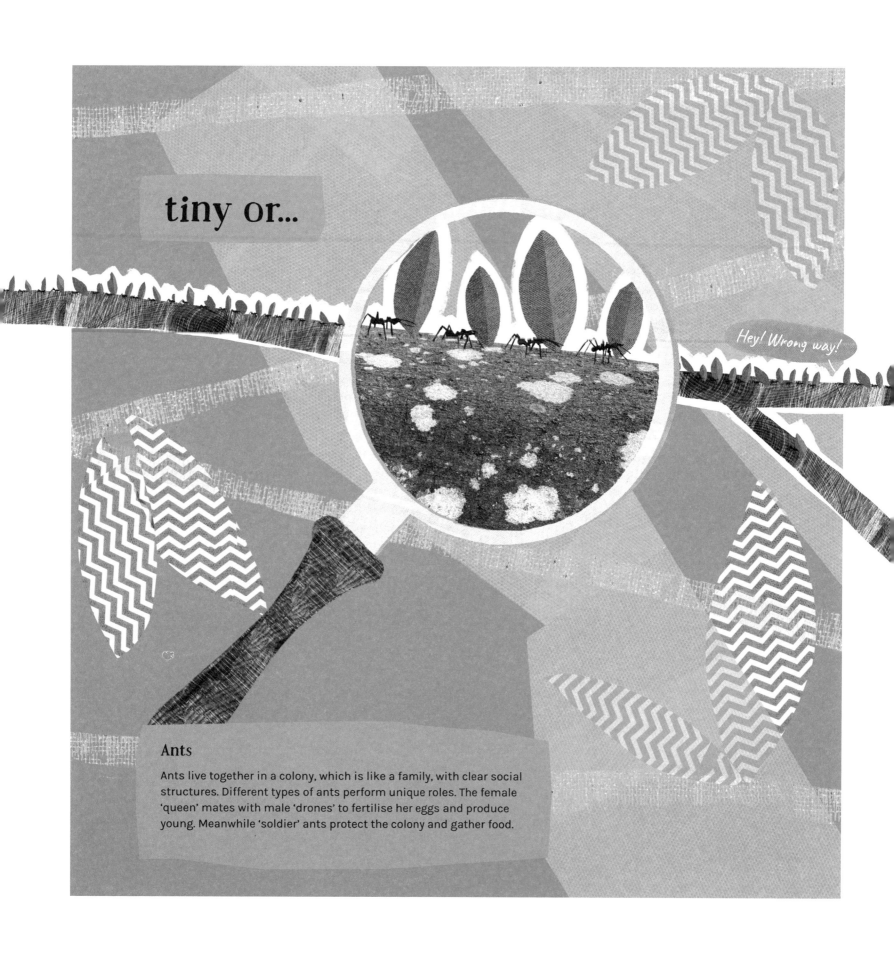

# tiny or...

Hey! Wrong way!

## Ants

Ants live together in a colony, which is like a family, with clear social structures. Different types of ants perform unique roles. The female 'queen' mates with male 'drones' to fertilise her eggs and produce young. Meanwhile 'soldier' ants protect the colony and gather food.

terrifically tall.

### Giraffes

A newborn giraffe is as tall as a human adult! Giraffes give birth standing up. Their calves arrive front feet first and have a drop of about two metres to reach the ground. This doesn't hurt them – it helps to open the fluid-filled sack they have grown in, and to detach the umbilical cord.

Perhaps you're
raised by one dad

or mum.

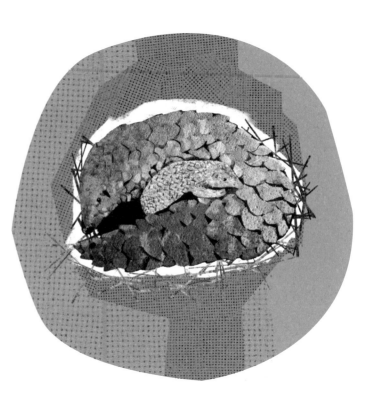

Or do others
help and...

# join the fun?

## Galapagos Sea Lions

Harems of Galapagos sea lions give birth together on a beach, watched over by one male. The females then share a nursery pool where they can leave their pups to play together while they go out to fish. The pups in the nursery are looked after by a group of female carers, each helping to raise the next generation safely together.

## Pangolins

Sometimes described as 'scaly anteaters', pangolins are solitary mammals who only come together to mate. Although some males may stay in the female's burrow for a short while, she will raise her pangopup alone. The pangolin is an attentive mother, carefully nursing her pup in her nesting burrow and curling protectively around it during sleep or times of danger. Pangolins are critically endangered due to poaching and habitat destruction.

## Elephants

Elephant mothers are supported by other females in the herd, as well as the herd's maternal grandmother. Together they all help to nurture and protect the baby calf. This sharing of care is known as 'alloparenting'. Baby elephants drink almost twenty pints of milk from their mother each day, and she must be on constant lookout to keep them safe. This is exhausting for any mother, so other support is important.

## Rheas

Rheas are large, flightless birds. The male incubates the eggs and raises chicks alone. He will brood eggs in his nest for around forty days, then take care of the chicks for up to six months, letting them shelter safely under his wings.

## Beavers

Male and female beavers form long-term pairs with only one partner, then rear their family together. The mother beaver nurses the young; the father looks after their territory; and both help to clean the kits' bedding. Later, both parents will forage for food for their young. Only around four per cent of mammals form monogamous pairs like this.

*Let's stick together*

# Your parents may work together

or take turns.

### Emperor Penguins

The female emperor penguin lays one egg, which is incubated by the male for up to seventy-five days whilst she heads back to sea to feed. When the female returns, the penguin parents then alternate between fishing at sea and caring for the chick on shore. Each parent goes away to sea for several weeks at a time.

You might make
your way alone

with no concerns.

### Sea Turtles

Female turtles lay their eggs in a nest of sand before returning to the sea. The eggs hatch around two months later and the baby turtles follow the bright light of the moon as they head towards the ocean to begin their own independent adventure.

# Your dad may love your daddy,

## your mummy might love Mum.

Eat up!

### Black Swans

A quarter of male black swans pair with other males, mating with a female simply to fertilise her eggs. Once the eggs have been laid, the female leaves, and the males hatch and rear the chicks together.

### Laysan Albatrosses

Over a third of female Laysan albatrosses pair with other females. It is common for albatross chicks to be brought up by two female birds, who make a long-term, exclusive partnership and share their care.

## Wattled Jacanas

Jacanas have many different mates, and the females pair with up to six male partners at once. This is to protect against high rates of egg loss to predators. The female will often set off to seek new mates while her previous male partner stays behind to hatch and rear existing chicks.

Partners may go and partners may come.

Perhaps your family
adopted you.

We've got this

## Adoption and fostering

Many animals nurture young that are not biologically their own – either from the same or different species. Animals can have a deep instinct to care for young and to form bonds of attachment and protection. Interspecies friendships also occur in the animal kingdom – friends can be family too.

**Maybe some you lost
or never knew.**

### Dragonfly

Dragonflies lay their eggs near water then flutter away, living
for just a few weeks longer. A dragonfly's life cycle ends while
their babies hatch and develop into nymphs underwater. After
several months or years, the nymphs transform into dragonflies,
emerging from the water to spread their own wings and fly.

You might feel drawn in...

*Ooh, cosy!*

**Grey Kangaroos**

A joey will live and nurse inside its mother's pouch for almost a year, taking frequent trips out to explore the world. Even after they leave the pouch, joeys may still squeeze back in for the occasional sip of milk!

or sometimes left out.

*Twit*

*Twoo*

**Tawny Owls**

Tawny owls are dedicated parents. But once their chicks become teenagers they encourage them to leave the nest and find their own territories with enough food to sustain them independently.

### Ring-Tailed Lemurs

Ring-tailed lemurs are tactile, social creatures. They live in large groups, or troops, and communicate with their bodies as well as voices. Cuddling up close and cleaning each other is a way of building up a strong bond and communicating feelings. Snuggling also helps them to keep warm and healthy. Due to deforestation and hunting, lemurs are one of the world's most endangered mammals.

*Purrrrrr*

## Your family may snuggle, or now and then shout.

*Chirp chirp*

*Cheep cheep*

### Zebra Finches

Zebra finch partners take turns to brood eggs, watch chicks and find food. But they sometimes use 'vocal negotiation' to quibble about their shared parental duties. If one is late coming back to the nest, its partner might call more shortly and more rapidly as if to say: 'You were gone for too long!'

Maybe Dad grew
and gave birth
to you?

### Seahorses

Male seahorses have a brood pouch on their tummy, into which a female lays eggs. The male then fertilises the eggs, closes the pouch, and becomes pregnant. After three weeks, he opens the pouch and squeezes out hundreds of tiny babies.

Or you feel tucked in with a sheltered view.

Room service please!

### Hornbills

After mating, hornbills seal their nest hole to keep their eggs and chicks safe from predators. A small opening is left, through which the male passes food. The eggs hatch inside the nest hole, with the chicks remaining inside until they are ready to break free and fly the nest.

Your mum may
lie low,

### Giant Pacific Octopus

The giant Pacific octopus lays one enormous clutch of eggs then carefully tends them for up to a year, keeping them clean and oxygenated. During this whole time, she will not leave her nest or feed herself, staying hidden in the shadows, keeping silent, cautious watch.

### Polar Bears

A polar bear gives birth to tiny cubs in a burrowed snow cave. Here she nurses them carefully until they are strong enough to travel with her back to the sea ice. At just a few months old, the cubs must make an epic journey, walking and swimming many miles a day, moving on constantly through treacherous terrain, to reach the place that offers food and sanctuary.

or go journeying.

There are
so many ways
of parenting.

But, however you start, once your wings have unfurled,

you'll find your true place
in this wide, wondrous world.

# Each Family is Unique

Every creature exists in its own special way. Some may feel strange to us – things that are unfamiliar can seem cute, or cruel, or even gruesome! But they have all evolved precisely to ensure the balance and survival of each extraordinary species. What's certain is that there's no such thing as 'normal', especially when it comes to rearing young...

### Some siblings squabble

Baby bald eagles often fight each other in the nest, competing for food and attention. The squabbles can be severe, but eagle parents rarely intervene.

### Some young need space

Tadpoles of the strawberry poison dart frog eat each other if they're left together. So the mother frog carries each one to its own separate pool of water, where it can grow alone. Once she's placed each tadpole in its own little pool, she visits it daily and lays it an egg to eat.

### Others need additional support

Chimpanzees make doting mothers. They nurse, groom and teach their infants for years, providing all the care they need. In Tanzania, one mother chimp let her daughter drink milk well beyond the typical weaning age because the infant was not able to eat solids. The mother also spent less time gathering her own food from trees so that she could carry her infant, who couldn't sit up alone or grip with her feet.

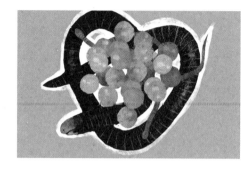

### Resources can be unexpected

Caecilians are worm-like amphibians that live in rainforests in underground burrows. Instead of lactating or foraging for food, some mother caecilians will feed their young by letting them lick a secretion from their body and bite off bits of their fatty skin. The mother re-grows this skin to keep her young fed.

### Family structures can shift

Cuckoos lay their eggs in other birds' nests. To avoid detection, they choose a host bird whose own eggs look similar – dunnocks or reed warblers are popular. Once the egg hatches, the host parents work hard to feed and successfully rear the cuckoo chick, ready for its first long flight from Europe to overwinter in Africa.

### We all need some protection

Adult scorpions have a hard outer shell. Females give birth to live babies. But the tiny scorplings' shells are initially so soft that it makes them an easy snack for predators. To protect her babies, the scorpion mother carries them all safely on her back – until their own protective casings have toughened.

### Life can hold threats

Female cheetahs raise their young alone. Every three or four days, the mother moves her litter of cubs to a new den. This is to keep them safe from harm by preventing a build-up of smell that predators might otherwise be able to track.

### Appearances can be deceptive

Alligators are known for being ferocious but give tender care to their infants. When alligator babies are ready to hatch, they make little 'umph, umph' noises from inside their eggs. Their mother then helps to open up the nest, before carrying her hatchlings gently in her mouth to the water. She will guard them closely for up to a year, rushing to protect her hatchlings whenever they signal distress.

## A little lift gets us started

Baby sea otters cannot swim for their first few months of life, even though they are born in the middle of the freezing ocean. They survive by balancing carefully on their mother's tummy until they learn to swim for themselves. A layer of warm, dry air in their special fur also helps them to float.

## Some parents go solo

Female stick insects can reproduce on their own without mating. This process is called 'parthenogenesis'. The female stick insect produces eggs that mature and then turn into female babies or 'nymphs'. If a male and female stick insect do mate, then there is a fifty per cent chance of some of the nymphs being male.

## Some parents can't stay long

Harp seals nurse their pups attentively to begin with, but after just twelve days, they return to sea and don't come back. Baby pups are left alone on the ice to fend for themselves. It will be another six weeks until they learn to swim and catch food for themselves. By this point they will have lost over half of their body weight, but hopefully were fed enough earlier on to survive.

## Parents can be devoted

A female mudskipper lays eggs in a chamber below the sand – safe from predators. The male mudskipper then keeps the chamber filled with oxygen – gulping air at the entrance to the chamber tunnel, swimming down, releasing the air, swimming back up – almost non stop until the eggs hatch.

## Some habits are a little smelly

At five or six months old, baby koalas start eating a special type of their mum's poo! This 'pap eating' helps the joeys to build up their gut bacteria, passed down via the poo, so that they are able to digest the fibrous leaves of the eucalyptus tree once they begin to wean off milk.

## Being different is natural

There is nothing on earth like a duckbill platypus – a venomous, swimming, egg-laying mammal. And platypus females feed their babies in a unique way too. They do not have any nipples, so once the 'puggles' hatch from their eggs, they suckle milk from tufts of their mother's fur where milk oozes out.

## It can take a village

Cotton-top tamarins parent collectively. Within the group, the lead female will give birth, usually to twins. After one week of care mainly from the mother, all of the females and males in the group will then take care of the babies and share responsibility with the mother. This species is critically endangered.

## Everybody hurts sometimes

Elephants seem to mourn their dead, undertaking a form of funeral ritual for their fallen and honouring their memory for years. From cows and chimpanzees to dolphins and giraffes – many animals express distress or grief when losing a group member they care for.

## Each baby is a miracle

The female panda only produces one egg a year, meaning there are just a few days when she can become pregnant – a tiny window of hope that makes each new cub even more miraculous. This, along with destruction of their habitat for farming and bamboo harvesting, is why fewer than 2000 giant pandas survive today.

Whoever you are, you're a miracle too – there will be nobody just like you! And as you grow up you'll find your own special way of being and of doing things. You may also discover the unique difference you can make to the world, and the ways in which we can all help these wild, wonderful creatures to keep on surviving on this planet that we share.

First paperback edition published in 2023

Edited by Emily Sharratt, in consultation
with Beth Cox, Inclusion and Equality Consultant

A catalogue record of this book is available from the British Library

ISBN 978-1-9997-704-3-3

Published by Doodles & Scribbles

www.doodlesandscribbles.co.uk
i: @doodlesandscribblesbooks
t: @doodlyscribbles
f: @doodlesandscribbles

# Design or colour in your own unique butterfly:

BE YOU!